——LUSCIOUS LOW-FAT——
MAIN DISHES

Jill Bradley

Sweetwater Press
Florence, Alabama

Published by Sweetwater Press
P.O. Box 1855
Florence, Alabama 35631

Produced by The Triangle Group, Ltd.
227 Park Avenue
Hoboken, NJ 07030

Design: Tony Meisel
Special thanks to Risa Gary of Mikasa, New York
Origination and printing: Cronion S.A., Barcelona

Printed in Spain

ISBN 1-884822-04-5

Contents

Introduction

Everyone loves a rich, satisfying main course. But current lifestyles make eating such food regularly a trying and fattening regime. Fear not! Satisfaction and taste have not disappeared forever. Hope lurks in these very pages. You can eat well and be satisfied without fat, heavy sauces and gobs of cream and butter.

Of course, part of the key to successful low-fat main courses is in the choice of ingredients. Fish, chicken and vegetables make the most logical starting point. Beef, lamb and veal are all high in cholesterol and fat and, though an occassional treat, should be avoided as a regular means of sustenance. Likewise, cream, butter, cheese, except in the smallest amounts, can spell disaster for any diet. Pork, as bred these days, is almost as low in fat as chicken, and can be turned into a wide variety of tempting dishes, especially when seasoned with *brio* and cooked in a manner appropriate for the cut of meat.

Most main course meat dishes should allow between 1/4 to 1/2 pound of meat per person, the more bone, the greater amount. And remember, a great deal can be done to fill people up with grains, vegetables, complex carbohydrates and accompaniments.

So eat hearty, but carefully.

Baked Whole Red Snapper

4-5 pound whole red snapper, split and cleaned
1 bunch scallions, finely chopped
1 teaspoon chopped garlic
1/2 teaspoon mixed peppercorns
1 cup sliced mushrooms
1 ripe tomato, coarsely chopped
1 teaspoon fresh thyme
2 tablespoons fresh lime juice
2 tablespoons low-fat margarine
freshly ground black pepper
1/2 cup white wine

Preheat the oven to 375 degrees F. Spray a roasting pan with low-calorie cooking spray; be sure the entire fish will fit in the pan.

Place the scallions, garlic, mixed peppercorns, mushrooms, tomatoes and thyme in the cavity of the fish. Sprinkle with lime juice and place 1 tablespoon of the margarine in the center. Skewer the fish closed.

Transfer the fish to the roasting pan. Cover the outside with freshly ground black pepper and place the remaining tablespoon of margarine on the top of the fish. Pour the wine over the fish.

Bake in the oven for 30-40 minutes or until firm. Baste every 10 minutes with pan juices. Serves 4.

Grilled Swordfish Steaks with Lemon Marinade

4 swordfish steaks, approximately 1 inch thick
2 tablespoons olive oil
4 tablespoons fresh lemon juice
1 1/2 teaspoons dried lemon peel
1 tablespoon coarsely ground black pepper

Place the swordfish steaks in a shallow dish large enough to hold them in a single layer. Pour the olive oil, lemon juice, lemon peel and black pepper over the fish. Using your fingers, turn the steaks several times to ensure that they are evenly coated. Let marinate at room temperature for at least 2 hours, turn occasionally.

Preheat the broiler or grill or prepare a charcoal grill. Spray broiler pan or grill with low-calorie cooking spray.

Grill the swordfish, 3 inches from the heat source for 3-5 minutes per side and golden. Cooking time will depend upon how well you like your fish cooked.

Grilled Skewered Sea Scallops

2 pounds sea scallops
3 tablespoons olive oil
1 tablespoon light soy sauce
1 tablespoon rice vinegar
1/2 cup chopped fresh cilantro
3 bell peppers; red, orange and yellow, cored,
    and sliced into chunks
1 yellow onion, coarsely chopped
1 box button mushrooms

In a large bowl, combine the olive oil, light soy sauce, rice vinegar and cilantro.Whisk to blend and add the sea scallops and turn several times until well coated. Allow mixture to marinate for 3 hours.

Preheat broiler or gas grill or prepare a charcoal grill. Spray grill or pan with low-calorie cooking spray.

Using 4 skewers, carefully arrange the scallops on the skewers, alternating them with the peppers, mushrooms and onions.

Grill, turning once, for 5 minutes or until done.
Serves 4.

Fresh Tuna in Lime-Ginger Marinade

1/2 cup fresh lime juice
2 cloves garlic, finely chopped
2 tablespoons olive oil
1 tablespoon vegetable oil
salt to taste, if desired
freshly ground black pepper
1 1/2 teaspoons finely chopped fresh ginger
6 tuna steaks, approximately 1 inch thick

Combine the lime juice, garlic, olive oil, vegetable oil, salt and pepper in a mixing bowl. Whisk until well blended.

Put the tuna steaks into a shallow dish large enough to hold them in one layer. Pour the marinade over the fish. Turn the steaks to coat well. Cover the dish and marinate in the refrigerator for 4 hours, turning occasionally.

Preheat broiler or gas grill or prepare a charcoal grill. Spray grill surface with low-calorie cooking spray.

Remove the tuna from the marinade. Reserve the marinade. Grill the steaks 3 inches from the heat until lightly browned, about 3-5 minutes per side.

Put reserved marinade into a saucepan and cook gently until heated through.

Arrange the tuna on a serving platter and pour hot marinade over the fish. Serves 4.

Sautéed Halibut with Celery & Peppers

1/2 cup natural almonds, coarsely chopped
4 halibut steaks, approximately 1 inch thick
freshly ground black pepper
flour for dredging
1 tablespoon low-fat margarine
2 tablespoons vegetable oil
2 peeled celery stalks, cut into 1 1/2 x 1/4 inch strips
1 sweet red pepper, cut into 1 1/2 x 1/4 inch strips

Preheat the oven to 350 degrees F. Place the chopped nuts on a baking sheet and toast in the oven for 5 minutes, stir once to turn. Remove from the oven and set aside.

Season the halibut steaks on both sides with pepper. Dredge the steaks in the flour and shake off any excess.

Melt the margarine and vegetable oil together in a large skillet over moderately high heat. Add the halibut and cook until lightly browned, about 4 minutes per side. Arrange the steaks on a serving platter large enough to hold them all in a single layer. Keep warm.

Add the celery and red pepper to the skillet. Cook, stirring constantly, until tender, about 5-6 minutes, only add more oil if necessary.

Spoon the celery and red pepper over the halibut. Sprinkle with the toasted almonds. Serves 4.

Chilled Mussels in Spicy Sauce

5 pounds mussels, scrubbed, cleaned and debearded
3/4 cup dry white wine
4 tablespoon olive oil
2 onions, very finely chopped
4 cloves garlic, minced
2 teaspoons ground cumin
2 pounds ripe tomatoes, peeled, seeded
    and finely chopped
2 35-ounce cans Italian plum tomatoes, drained
    and finely chopped
4 4-inch hot green chili peppers, seeded
    and finely chopped (wear rubber gloves)
1/4 cup finely chopped scallions
1/4 cup finely chopped fresh coriander

Put the wine into a heavy pot and add the mussels. Cover the pot and steam over high heat until the mussels open, about 5-8 minutes. Discard any mussels that do not open.

Using a slotted spoon, transfer the mussels to a large, shallow baking dish. Reserve the liquid. Remove the top shells from the mussels and discard them. Loosen the mussels from the lower shells, but leave them in the shells. Loosely cover the dish with damp paper towels and plastic wrap. Refrigerate for 4 hours or overnight.

Strain the reserved liquid into a bowl through a sieve lined with a double thickness of cheesecloth. Set aside.

Heat the olive oil in a skillet. When hot, add the onions and cook over a moderate heat until softened, about 5 minutes. Add the garlic and cook, stirring constantly until softened, about 2-3 minutes longer. Sprinkle the cumin over the onion and garlic, cook 1 minute longer, stir twice. Add the fresh tomatoes, canned tomatoes and 3/4 cup of the reserved cooking liquid. Bring the mixture to a boil. Reduce the heat and simmer, stirring constantly, until the sauce has thickened slightly, about 10 minutes.

Add the chili peppers and scallions, stir well. Remove from the heat and let the sauce cool. Add the chopped coriander and stir well.

Remove the mussels from the refrigerator and arrange on four individual serving plates. Spoon the sauce into individual bowls and serve with the mussels for dipping. Serves 4.

Codfish with Crunchy Herb Coating

2 pounds codfish fillets
1/4 cup finely chopped pecans
1 cup bread crumbs
1 tablespoon chopped tarragon
freshly ground black pepper
2 tablespoons low-fat milk
1 tablespoon Dijon style mustard

Preheat the oven to 400 degrees F. Line a baking sheet with aluminum foil and grease it with low-calorie cooking spray.

Place the pecans on a separate baking dish and toast in the oven for 3-5 minutes or until golden. Remove and allow to cool. Combine the pecans and bread crumbs, tarragon and black pepper.

Combine the milk and mustard in a small bowl. Brush the fish on both sides with the mixture. Dip each codfish fillet evenly into the bread crumb mixture, place on the baking sheet.

Bake in the oven for 15 minutes or until fish flakes easily and is golden. Serves 4.

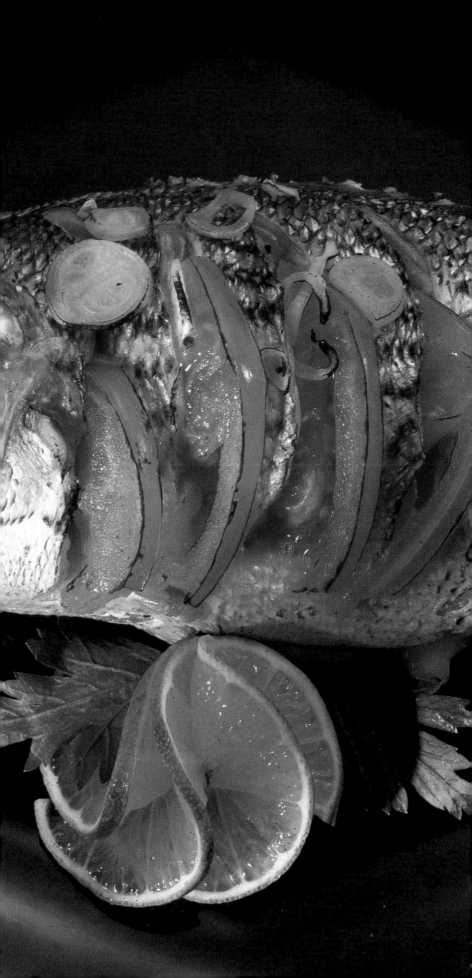

Striped Bass with Fennel

5 small fennel bulbs, trimmed (reserve trimmings)
    and halved
1 5-pound cleaned whole striped bass
1 tablespoon walnut oil
2 teaspoons coarse salt
2 large onions, thickly sliced
2 large tomatoes, thickly sliced and seeded
1 cup dry white wine or dry vermouth
2 cups evaporated milk, lightly beaten
4 tablespoons low-fat margarine
2 tablespoons minced fennel fronds
salt to taste, if desired
lemon wedges for garnish
fennel fronds for garnish

Preheat the oven to 400 degrees F.

    Gently pat the fish dry. Rub it inside and out with the walnut oil and sprinkle inside and out with the coarse salt. Measure the thickness of the fish to determine its cooking time. Stuff the cavity of the fish with the reserved fennel trimmings.

    Line a large roasting pan with a piece of aluminum foil folded in half lengthwise. Put the fish on the foil. Arrange the onion and tomato slices on top of the fish, held in place with wooden toothpicks. Arrange the fennel bulbs around the fish and add the wine. Cover the pan securely with a piece of aluminum foil. Bake for 9 minutes per inch of thickness or until the fish is just opaque.

    While the fish cooks, boil the evaporated milk in a saucepan until it is reduced to 1 cup. Remove from the heat. Remove the fish from the oven. Remove the toothpicks and tomatoes and onions. Discard the onions. Chop the tomatoes finely and set aside. Reserve the pan juices.

    Transfer the fish to a serving platter and keep warm. Arrange the fennel bulbs around the fish.

    Strain the pan juices through a sieve into a saucepan. Discard any solids remaining in the sieve. Bring the pan juices to a boil and continue to boil until the sauce is reduced to about 1 3/4 cups.

    Remove the sauce from the heat and whisk in the margarine, 1/2 tablespoon at a time. Season with salt, if desired and pour into a sauce boat. Serves 8-10.

Roast Chicken

1 4-pound roasting chicken
1 teaspoon chopped garlic in oil
2 teaspoons fresh rosemary
coarsely ground black pepper
1 tablespoon olive oil
1 tablespoon sesame oil
1 large onion, coarsely chopped
4 rosemary sprigs
4 cloves of garlic, peeled
freshly ground black pepper

Preheat the oven to 350 degrees F. Have a roasting pan and rack ready.

In a small bowl combine the chopped garlic, 2 teaspoons of rosemary, black pepper, olive oil, and sesame oil; blend well. Reserve.

Clean the chicken, rinse and pat dry, remove all a visible fat. Stuff the cavity of the bird with the onion, rosemary sprigs, and garlic; skewer closed.

Using a brush, cover the outside of the chicken with the garlic oil mixture; if anything remains in the bowl, put it on with your hands. Carefully transfer to the roasting rack.

Roast in the oven for 1 1/4-1 1/2 hours or until the chicken tests done.

Remove from the oven and let rest for at least 15 minutes before carving.

Remove the skewers and spoon out the onion garlic mixture; serve in a separate bowl. Serves 6.

Chicken Sautéed with Lemon & Herbs

2 tablespoons finely chopped lemon rind
1/2 cup fresh lemon juice
4 tablespoons olive oil
1/2 cup dry white wine
1 teaspoon honey
salt to taste
freshly ground black pepper
1/4 cup finely chopped fresh rosemary, thyme and
    oregano, combined or 1 1/2 teaspoons each dried
    rosemary, thyme and oregano
4 large whole chicken breasts, skinned, boned and
    halved, all visible fat removed
2 tablespoons low fat margarine
6 tablespoons evaporated milk, if desired

In a small bowl combine the lemon rind, lemon juice,
2 tablespoons olive oil, white wine, honey, salt, pepper,
rosemary, thyme and oregano. Mix well.

Put the chicken breasts into a large shallow dish.
Pour the marinade over the pieces and turn to coat well.
Cover and refrigerate for 4-6 hours, turning occasionally.

Remove the chicken from the marinade and gently
pat dry. Reserve marinade.

Melt the margarine in a large skillet over medium-
high heat. Add the chicken breasts and sauté until golden
brown, about 5-7 minutes per side. Remove the chicken
from the skillet and keep warm on a plate.

Pour off the liquid from the skillet. Add the reserved
marinade and bring the mixture to a boil. Continue to boil
until the marinade is reduced to 1/2 cup. Add the evaporated milk, only if a thicker sauce is desired. If you add
the milk, boil for 3 minutes longer.

Return the chicken to the skillet. Cook until the
chicken is heated through. Serve the chicken on a platter
with the sauce poured over it. Serves 4-6.

Grilled Chicken with Mustard-Herb Coating

1 3-pound chicken, cut into serving pieces, skin
    and all visible fat removed
4 tablespoons olive oil
1 tablespoon chopped garlic in oil
2 tablespoon lemon juice
1 tablespoon fresh rosemary
coarsely ground black pepper

Place the chicken in a bowl. In a separate bowl combine
the olive oil, garlic, lemon juice, rosemary and black
pepper, whisk to blend.

Season chicken with black pepper. Pour marinade
over chicken and turn until well coated. Cover bowl and
marinate at room temperature for 3-4 hours. Turn twice.

Preheat the broiler or gas grill or prepare a charcoal
grill. Spray the grill pan with low-calorie cooking spray.

Grill the chicken 3 inches from the heat source for
20-30 minutes or until done. Turn occasionally. Serves 4.

Chicken Sautéed in Red Wine

3 pounds chicken breasts, boneless, skinless,
    all visible fat removed
flour for dredging
salt to taste, if desired
pepper to taste
2 cloves garlic, chopped
1 large yellow onion, sliced
1 cup quartered mushrooms
1/2 cup red wine
1 tablespoon chopped fresh oregano

Cut the chicken breasts into bite-size pieces. Season the flour with salt and pepper, dredge chicken pieces lightly in flour.

In a non-stick skillet, sprayed lightly with low-calorie cooking spray, sauté the chicken until lightly brown on all sides, about 5 minutes.

In a large pot combine the garlic, onion, mushrooms, red wine, oregano and the chicken. Bring the mixture to a boil, lower the heat and cook for 40-45 minutes or until chicken is very tender. Serves 4.

Chicken in Yogurt Marinade

1 3-pound chicken, skinned and cut into serving pieces,
    with all visible fat removed
1 16 ounce container low-fat yogurt
1 tablespoon chopped garlic in oil
1/2 cup chopped fresh mint

In a large bowl combine the yogurt, garlic and mint, add
the chicken and turn several times until well coated.
Cover and allow to marinate for 3-5 hours, turn occasionally.

Preheat broiler or gas grill or prepare a charcoal grill.
Spray grill or pan with low-calorie cooking spray.

Remove the chicken from the marinade. Grill chicken
3 inches from the heat source, turning often, for 40
minutes or until done. Serves 4.

Chicken with Olives & Herbs

1-3 pound chicken, cut into 8 pieces, skinned,
    all visible fat removed
freshly ground black pepper
salt, if desired
1 large white onion, sliced
1 red pepper, cored and thinly sliced
1 yellow pepper, cored and thinly sliced
2 cloves of garlic, minced
1 large can imported Italian plum tomatoes,
    coarsely chopped, reserve liquid
1/2 cup low-fat chicken broth
2 tablespoons chopped fresh basil
5 green olives, in brine, pitted
5 black olives, in brine, pitted
1/4 cup red wine

Season the chicken pieces with pepper and salt. Spray a large non-stick skillet with low-calorie cooking spray, heat the skillet and add the chicken. Cook until chicken is brown on all sides, about 5 minutes. Remove the chicken from the skillet and set aside.

Add the onion, peppers and garlic, cook over a medium heat for approximately 5 minutes. Add the tomatoes and the reserved liquid, the chicken broth, basil, olives and red wine. Bring the mixture to a boil, reduce the heat and allow the mixture to simmer for 3 minutes.

Return the chicken to the skillet and cover. Simmer for 30-40 minute or until the chicken is tender. Serves 4.

Chicken-Ginger Sauté

4 boneless chicken breasts, all skin
    and visible fat removed
salt to taste, if desired
freshly ground black pepper
flour (for dredging)
2 tablespoons olive or vegetable oil
2 finely chopped shallots
2 whole scallions, thinly sliced
2 cloves garlic, minced
2 1/2 tablespoons finely chopped fresh ginger
1/4 cup white wine
1/4 cup light soy sauce

Put each chicken breast between two sheets of waxed
paper. With a meat tenderizer or the flat side of a heavy
cleaver, gently pound the chicken until it is 1/4 inch thick.
Season each piece with salt and pepper and dredge lightly
in flour. Shake off any excess.

In a large non-stick skillet heat the oil over a medium
heat. Add the chicken breasts and sauté until they are
lightly browned, about 2-3 minutes per side. Remove the
chicken from the skillet, keep warm.

Add the shallots, scallions and garlic to the skillet.
Sauté until softened, about 5 minutes. Add the ginger,
white wine and soy sauce to the skillet. Simmer, stirring
constantly for 2-3 minutes.

Return the chicken breasts to the skillet and cook just
until heated through, about 1-2 minutes. Serve with sauce
spooned over the chicken or on the side. Serves 4.

Turkey with Garlic, Lemon & Parsley

2 boneless turkey breasts, cut into 2-inch pieces
1/2 cup fresh lemon juice
1 tablespoon olive or vegetable oil
3 cloves garlic, chopped
1/2 cup finely chopped Italian parsley
coarsely ground black pepper

In a large bowl combine the lemon juice, oil, garlic, parsley and pepper, whisk until well blended. Add turkey cubes and turn several times until well coated. Cover and let marinate for 3 hours.

Remove turkey from marinade. Reserve marinade.

Heat a large non-stick skillet, add as many turkey pieces as will fit in one layer and sauté until lightly browned on all sides, about 5 minutes. Remove from pan and keep warm. If there are additional turkey cubes, sauté as above.

Add the reserved marinade to the skillet and quickly bring the mixture to a boil. Return the turkey to the skillet and cover, reduce heat. Cook for 3-5 minutes or until turkey is tender. Serve with sauce. Serves 6.

Turkey Marsala

1 pound turkey cutlets
salt to taste, if desired
coarsely ground black pepper
1 tablespoon olive oil
1/2 cup chopped onion
1/2 cup sliced button mushrooms
1 teaspoon chopped garlic in oil
3/4 cup Marsala

Season the turkey with salt and pepper. Lightly dredge
in flour, shake off any excess.

Heat a large non-stick skillet. Sauté as many cutlets as
will fit in the skillet in a single layer. Sauté until lightly
browned on both sides, approximately 5 minutes, turn
once. Remove from the skillet and keep warm. Repeat
with remaining cutlets.

Add the olive oil to the skillet and heat. Add the
onions, mushrooms and garlic, sauté until the onions are
translucent, about 5 minutes. Remove from the skillet and
keep warm.

Add the Marsala to the skillet and cook over a high
heat, for 2 minutes. Add the turkey cutlets along with the
mushroom-onion mixture to the Marsala. Lower the heat
and continue to cook until all ingredients are heated
through, about 2-3 minutes. Serves 4.

Turkey-Tomato Stew

3 pounds turkey pieces, light and dark meat,
    skin and fat removed
salt if desired
freshly ground pepper
2 cloves garlic, finely chopped
1 large white onion, sliced
1 large can imported Italian plum tomatoes, retain liquid
coarsely ground black pepper
1 bay leaf
1 teaspoon chopped oregano
8 ounces small button mushrooms, washed and halved
1/2 cup red wine

Season the turkey pieces with salt and pepper. Heat a large non-stick skillet, add the turkey and cook until light brown on all sides, about 5 minutes. Remove from the pan and set aside.

Add the garlic and onions to the skillet, cook until onions have softened and are translucent, remove from the heat.

In a large stock pot combine the turkey pieces, onion and garlic, tomatoes with their liquid, black pepper, bay leaf, oregano, mushrooms and wine. Cook over a moderate to low heat for 45-50 minutes or until turkey is tender. Serves 6.

Turkey Curry

3 tablespoons low-fat margarine
1 large white onion, chopped
1 Granny Smith apple, peeled, cored and chopped
2 cloves garlic, chopped
1/2 cup raisins
1/4 cup chopped non-salted cashews
1/4 cup flour
1 tablespoon curry powder
1 1/2 cups low-fat yogurt
3 cups cubed cooked turkey

Melt the margarine in a large skillet, add the onion, apple and garlic, sauté for 5 minutes. Add the raisins and cashews, continue to cook for 1 minute longer.

In a small bowl mix the flour and the curry powder, add to the skillet, stir well and cook for 2 minutes.

Add the yogurt and over a low heat stir until well blended. Simmer for 3 minutes or until sauce begins to thicken.

Add turkey, stir well. Cook until turkey is heated, approximately 5 minutes. Serve over brown rice.
Serves 4.

Pork Chops with Apples & Prunes

4 thick center-cut pork chops, all visible fat removed
2/3 cup white wine
1/2 cup low-fat chicken broth
1 Granny Smith apple, peeled, cored and thinly sliced
1 medium white onion, finely chopped
1/2 cup pitted prunes
1/2 teaspoon ground cardamom
freshly ground pepper to taste

Heat a large non-stick skillet, add the pork chops and cook until golden on both sides, approximately 3-5 minutes per side. Remove from the pan and keep warm.

Add the wine and chicken broth to the skillet, cook over a moderate heat for 2 minutes. Add the apple, onion and prunes, cook uncovered for 3-5 minutes or until apples and onions are soft.

Return the pork chops to the skillet and over a low heat cook for an additional 2-3 minutes or until the pork is heated through. Serves 4.

Pork Chops Braised with Scallions

6 loin pork chops
salt to taste, if desired
freshly ground black pepper
1 cup thinly sliced scallions
1 teaspoon chopped garlic in oil
1 cup water
1 cup low-fat chicken broth
2 tablespoons white vermouth
2 tablespoons fresh thyme

Season the pork chops with the salt and pepper.

Heat a large skillet, add the pork chops and cook over a medium heat for 2-3 minutes per side or until chops are browned. Turn occasionally.

Add the scallions, garlic, water and chicken broth, quickly bring the mixture to a boil. Reduce the heat, cover and gently simmer for 20-30 minutes or until pork is very tender.

Remove the chops from the skillet and keep warm. Add the vermouth and thyme to the skillet and simmer for 2 minutes. Pour over the chops and serve. Serves 6.

Warm Scallop Salad

2 ripe tomatoes
2 tablespoons olive oil
2 shallots, finely chopped
2 tablespoons fresh lime juice
1/2 teaspoon salt
1 teaspoon freshly ground pepper
2 tablespoons finely chopped fresh basil
1 pound sea scallops
freshly ground pepper, to taste
salt, if desired, to taste
2 bunches arugula, washed and stemmed

Halve and seed the tomatoes. Chop finely and set aside.

Heat the olive oil in a skillet over a medium heat. Add the shallots and sauté until soft, about 2-3 minutes. Stir in the lime juice, salt and pepper. Remove the skillet from the heat and add the tomatoes and basil. Stir well and set dressing aside.

Rinse and gently dry the scallops. Cut very large scallops in half.

Heat a large non-stick skillet. Add the scallops and sauté, turning frequently, for 3-5 minutes. Remove from the skillet and put the scallops into a large mixing bowl.

Add half the dressing to the warm scallops and season with additional salt and pepper. Toss well.

Distribute the arugula evenly among 4 plates. Top each plate with a portion of the warm scallops. Drizzle additional dressing over each portion. Serves 4.

Curried Chicken Salad

4 chicken breasts, skinned and boned,
    all visible fat removed
2 tablespoons olive or vegetable oil
1 cup low-fat plain yogurt
1/8 cup curry powder
salt to taste, if desired
freshly ground pepper, to taste
1/2 pound seedless green grapes
1 cup julienned dried apricots
1 cup drained mandarin orange sections
1/4 cup apricot liqueur
1 head leafy lettuce, washed and dried

Cut the chicken breasts into 1-inch cubes.

Heat the olive oil in a skillet. Add chicken and cook over a moderate heat, turning often, until cubes are firm but brown, about 7-10 minutes. Using a slotted spoon transfer the chicken to a mixing bowl.

In a small bowl combine the yogurt and curry powder. Mix well. Add the mixture to the chicken. Season with salt and pepper, add more curry if desired.

Add grapes, apricots, orange sections and apricot liqueur to the chicken. Toss until all the ingredients are well coated. Chill for at least 1 hour.

Line a serving dish with the lettuce leaves. Mound the chicken on the lettuce and serve. Serves 4-6.

Chicken Salad with Green Peppercorn Dressing

2 cups cooked cubed chicken, white meat only
4 tablespoons olive or vegetable oil
2 tablespoons tarragon vinegar
1 tablespoons crushed green peppercorns
4 large very ripe tomatoes

Place the chicken in a large mixing bowl.

In a small jar or bowl combine the oil, vinegar and peppercorns, mix well.

Wash and cut the tops of the tomatoes. Scoop out the insides, coarsely chop and add to the chicken. Shake or mix the dressing again and pour over the chicken-tomato mixture.

Spoon mixture into tomato shells and serve with a green salad. Serves 4.

Mussel, Spinach & Mushroom Salad

1 pound button mushrooms
1 tablespoon lemon juice
1 clove garlic, finely chopped
1 teaspoon Dijon-style mustard
2 tablespoons tarragon vinegar
1/4 cup olive oil
1 tablespoon fresh thyme
1 pound fresh spinach, washed and torn
5 pounds mussels, scrubbed and beards removed
1 cup white wine
1 cup water
2 cloves garlic, chopped

Clean and thinly slice the mushrooms. Place them in a mixing bowl, sprinkle with lemon juice.

In a small jar combine the garlic, mustard, vinegar and oil, shake very well. Pour over the mushrooms, and sprinkle with the thyme. Toss well and marinate for 1 hour.

Place the mussels in a large pot, add the wine, water and garlic; bring the mixture to a boil. Cover, reduce the heat and steam for 5 minutes or until all the mussels open, stir twice to help distribute mussels. Drain and discard any mussels that have not opened. Shell mussels and allow to cool. Transfer to mixing bowl.

Drain the mushrooms, reserving the marinade.

Add the mushrooms and spinach to the mussels, toss with the reserved marinade. Transfer to serving bowl. Serves 4.

Grilled Tuna &
White Bean Salad

1 1/2 pounds fresh tuna
1/2 cup fresh lime juice
2 teaspoons chopped garlic in oil
1 tablespoon fresh thyme
coarsely ground black pepper
1 large red onion, sliced thin
1 large can small white beans, rinsed and drained

Dressing:
4 tablespoons olive or vegetable oil
2 tablespoons tarragon vinegar
1 teaspoon Dijon-style mustard
1 clove garlic, minced
freshly ground black pepper

In a shallow dish combine the lime juice, garlic and thyme; stir to mix. Add the tuna turning several times to coat; sprinkle with coarsely ground black pepper. Allow the fish to marinate for at least 3 hours.

Preheat the broiler or gas grill or prepare a charcoal grill. Spray grill surface with low-fat cooking spray. Grill the tuna, 3 inches from heat source, for 3-5 minutes per side or until done. Remove from the grill and allow to cool to lukewarm.

Cut the tuna into large chunks and place in a serving bowl. Add the sliced red onion and drained white beans.

In a small jar or bowl combine the oil, vinegar, mustard, garlic and pepper, shake or mix well. Pour over tuna mixture and toss. Serve over or with greens if desired. Serves 4.

Cold Beef Salad

2 pounds top sirloin steak, all visible fat removed
freshly ground black pepper to taste
salt, if desired
1 red bell pepper, thinly sliced
1 yellow bell pepper thinly sliced
1 green bell pepper, thinly sliced
10 scallions, thinly sliced
1 1/2 cup low-fat yogurt or low-fat mayonnaise
2 cloves garlic, chopped
1 teaspoon drained prepared white horseradish

Preheat broiler or gas grill or prepare a charcoal grill.
    Season the steak on both sides with pepper and salt.
Grill the steak until it is medium rare, about 7-10 minutes
per side. When done, remove the steak from the grill and
cool completely. When cool, cut into thin strips.
    In a large bowl combine the steak strips, red, yellow
and green peppers, scallions, yogurt or mayonnaise,
garlic and horseradish. Season with additional pepper.
Toss until all ingredients are well coated. Cover the bowl
and chill for 3-4 hours. Remove from the refrigerator
30 minutes before serving. Serve on or with greens if
desired. Serves 4.